92

The Rain Forest

The Remarkable Rain Forest

Mae Woods
ABDO Publishing Company

visit us at
www.abdopub.com

Published by Abdo Publishing Company 4940 Viking Drive, Edina, Minnesota 55435.
Copyright © 1999 by Abdo Consulting Group, Inc. International copyrights reserved in all countries. No part of this book may be reproduced in any form without written permission from the publisher.

Printed in the United States.

Photo credits: Peter Arnold, Inc.

Edited by Lori Kinstad Pupeza
Contributing editor Morgan Hughes
Graphics by Linda O'Leary

Library of Congress Cataloging-in-Publication Data

Woods, Mae.
      The remarkable rain forest / Mae Woods.
      p. cm. -- (The rain forest)
      Includes index.
      Summary: Surveys the location, weather, products, plants, and animals of rain forests.
      ISBN 1-57765-021-2
      1. Rain forests--juvenile literature. 2. Rain forest ecology--Juvenile literature. [1. Rain forests.] I. Title. II. Series: Woods, Mae. Rain forest.
      QH86.W66 1999
      577.34--dc21   98-15374
                                                             CIP
                                                             AC

Note to reader
The words in the text that are the color green refer to the words in the glossary.

Contents

What Are Rain Forests?

Rain forests are the jungle regions located on either side of the equator. These areas are also called the tropics because most lie between the Tropic of Cancer and the Tropic of Capricorn. Millions of years ago rain forests covered most of the earth, including land that is now the United States. This is where dinosaurs once lived.

Today, there aren't as many rain forests, but they are home to many kinds of plants and animals. The weather is warm, and it rains nearly every day. Many species could not live anywhere else. The special climate allows plants to

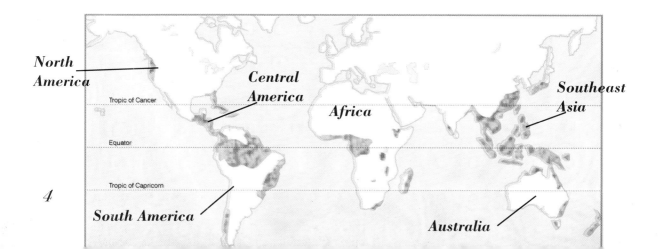

North America

Central America

Africa

Southeast Asia

Tropic of Cancer

Equator

Tropic of Capricorn

South America

Australia

grow all year long. Animals can always find food to eat. They can always find leaves to build fresh nests in the trees.

Most rain forests are located in three areas of the world: in Central and South America, in Africa, and in Southeast Asia.

An orchid in the Malaysian rain forest.

Amazonia

South America has the world's largest rain forest. This area is known as Amazonia because the mighty Amazon River flows through it. Amazonia stretches across Brazil to Peru, Bolivia, Colombia, and Ecuador. Many small rivers run into the Amazon. During heavy rains, the river may rise as high as a two-story house. People who live there build their homes on stilts.

In the mountains of Brazil, the treetops are covered in rainy, white mist. They appear to be in the clouds. These regions are called cloud forests.

In Colombia, more than half the rain forest is protected. No one is allowed to cut down the trees. There, native people live in ways that do not harm plants or animals.

There are also rain forests in the Caribbean and Central America. They can be found in Puerto Rico,

Brazil

Atlantic
Ocean

the U.S. Virgin Islands, Guatemala, Honduras, Nicaragua, Belize, Costa Rica, and Panama.

A flooded forest in the Amazonian rain forest.

African Rain Forests

On the continent of Africa, rain forests are found along the west coast and in Cameroon, Congo, Gabon, and Zaire. A few groups of native people still live in these jungles. One group, the Pygmies, are nomads. This means that they move their homes to new camps every few weeks. They settle where they find ripe fruit, fresh water, and wild animals to hunt.

Many African animals such as mountain gorillas and elephants are now rare. In recent years, people have set aside land reserves to protect these special animals and to preserve the trees and plants.

There are also rain forests on the island of Madagascar, which is east of Africa. Many species of plants and animals are unique to this area. The lemur, a large eyed, fluffy animal related to the monkey is found here. A valuable plant called the rosy periwinkle was discovered here. Its leaves are used to make a medicine for treating leukemia and Hodgkin's disease.

Africa

Atlantic Ocean

Madagascar

A mountain stream in an African rain forest.

Southeast Asian Rain Forests

*R*ain forests once covered most of Southeast Asia. Over the years, many jungle regions have been cut down. The trees were cleared away by loggers or farmers to build towns. Today, there are still rain forests in Thailand, along the southern coast of Southeast Asia. Rain forests also can be found in the island countries of Malaysia, Indonesia, Borneo, New Guinea, and the Philippines. Australia also has regions of rain forests.

Some island people have always lived in isolation. They have not learned new ways of life. They still use stone tools and simple weapons just as their people did hundreds of years ago.

The islands in these tropical areas are often hit by storms. Rain forest trees act as a buffer to hurricanes. The trees help to block or slow the fierce winds. Without them, the storms would travel to other countries and do much more damage.

Southeast Asia

Indian Ocean

A Rafflesia flower in the Malaysian rain forest.

Weather

The rain forests have more wet weather than any other area of land in the world. There are two seasons: a long season of heavy rains and a short season of light rains. The rain is put to good use in the tropics. Some of it runs into rivers and streams, adding fresh nutrients to the water.

Most of it is soaked up by trees and plants. A large tree can take in many quarts of water through its roots each day. Then the leaves of the tree release the moisture back into the air. This moisture, from thousands of plants, forms clouds that make more rain. About half of the rain that falls in the tropics is returned to the earth as new showers.

The temperature in a rain forest stays about 80 degrees Fahrenheit (26 degrees Celsius) all year. This warm, moist climate is perfect for plant growth.

A misty Philippine rain forest.

Products

*P*lants in the rain forests provide the world with food, spices, medicine, and many other products. Rubber is an important product that was discovered in the Amazon. It is made from latex, a sap found inside rubber trees. Latex is collected by cutting into the bark and letting the sap drip out. The tree is not harmed by this. It continues to grow and produce more latex. Rubber is a renewable resource.

The rain forest trees include many beautiful hardwoods such as teak, mahogany, balsa, and ebony. These trees are not a renewable resource. If they are cut down, new trees will not grow for a long time. The soil that these trees grow in washes away easily.

Oils used to make perfume and other products come from the flowers, leaves, or seeds of certain rain forest plants. Citronella, sandalwood, and patchouli are some of these oils that add unique smells to soaps, shampoo, and candles.

The sap from this tree can be made into rubber.

Foods

Sugar cane, ginger, cinnamon, nutmeg, peppercorns, vanilla beans, coffee, tea, cocoa, rice, oranges, mangoes, bananas, pineapples, avocados, yams, and many kinds of nuts were first discovered in the rain forests. Chicle, which is used to make chewing gum, comes from the sap of a plant found in Belize and Guatemala. Now, most of these foods are grown on farms in many different countries.

There are some weird fruits and vegetables in the rain forest that still have not been discovered by the rest of the world. This is beginning to change. Starfruit, also called carambola, is now exported outside the tropics. There are many other exotic foods from the rain forest that may appear in our markets someday soon. They have odd shapes and strange, colorful names, such as pummelo, soursop, naranjilla, mangosteen, breadfruit, and rambutan. Wouldn't you like to taste them?

This man is harvesting latex, which is a source of chicle. Chicle is used to make chewing gum.

17

Medicine

*F*or many years, scientists have been studying how native peoples make medicine from rain forest plants. Important drugs have been made based on native cures. Medicine that helps to treat malaria was found in a rain forest. Quinine, made from the bark of a tree in Peru, helps to control one of the world's most deadly diseases.

Curare is a sticky poison made by mixing together the sap of two vines. Hunters put it on the tips of their arrows. When curare goes under the skin of an animal, its muscles stop working. The animal cannot move. After studying curare, doctors were able to make a drug like it to relax patients' muscles.

Another medicine was discovered by studying poisonous frogs. A drug based on the medicine found is now used to make patients sleep during surgery.

Opposite page: Cinchona
is a source of quinine.

Unusual Animals

Many strange creatures live in rain forests. Some look as though their body parts were mixed up with another animal. The okapi has striped legs like a zebra, but the rest of its body is brown. The tree kangaroo has a long, grasping tail like a monkey. They like to live alone and eat lots of leaves. The lemur, a squirrel-sized tree animal, has hands like a human with fingerprints, fingernails, and a thumb. The pig-like tapir has a snout shaped like a small elephant trunk.

There are animals in the rain forests that have unusual physical skills. Two types of lizards, the gecko and the chameleon, are able to change the color of their skin. The chameleon can move its eyes in different directions at the same time. The sloth, a slow-moving tree animal, can hang upside down all day, even when it's asleep. The cassowary is a bird from Australia that cannot fly. It fights off its enemies by kicking them.

This flap-necked
chameleon is found
in the rain forest.

Glossary

Climate - the usual weather conditions.

Damage - harm or injury.

Equator (e-KWAY-tor) - the imaginary line around the center of the earth.

Exported - sent from one country to another.

Hodgkin's disease - a cancer of the lymph nodes and lymphatic system.

Hurricane (HER-ee-kane) - a very strong windstorm, often with heavy rain.

Isolation (i-so-LAY-shune) - set apart from others.

Latex - a milky white substance that can be made into rubber or gum.

Leukemia (loo-KEE-mee-uh) - a form of cancer that affects the blood.

Malaria (mah-LARE-e-a) - a disease caused by the bite of certain mosquitoes.

Moisture - water that is in the air or that forms tiny drops on a surface.

Native people - born in or belonging in a natural way to a certain region.

Nutrients (new-TREE-ints) - the matter that plants and animals need in order to grow.

Pygmy (PIG-me) - people of equatorial Africa who are under 5 feet (1.5m) tall.

Quinine - a substance made from the bark of the cinchona tree.

Region - an area or place.

Renewable resource- a useful product that can be used again.

Species (SPEE-sheez) - a group of plants or animals that are alike in certain ways.

Surgery (SIR-jah-ree) - an operation to treat a disease or injury.

Tropics - warm areas of the earth between the Tropic of Cancer and the Tropic of Capricorn near the equator.

Unique (u-NEEK)- special; one of a kind.

Internet Sites

Amazon Interactive
http://www.eduweb.com/amazon.html
Explore the geography of the Ecuadorian rain forest through on-line games and activities. Discover the ways that the Quichua live off the land. Then try your hand at running a community-based ecotourism project along the Río Napo.

Living Edens: Manu, Peru's Hidden Rainforest
http://www.pbs.org/edens/manu/
This site is about the animals and indigenous people who populate Peru's Manu region.

The Rain Forest Workshop
http://kids.osd.wednet.edu/Marshall/rainforest_home_page.html
The Rain Forest Workshop was developed by Virginia Reid and the students at Thurgood Marshall Middle School, in Olympia, Washington. This site is one of the best school sites around with links to many other sites as well as great information on the rain forest.

The Tropical Rain Forest in Suriname
http://www.euronet.nl/users/mbleeker/suriname/suri-eng.html
A multimedia tour through the rainforest in Suriname (SA). Read about plants, animals, Indians, and Maroons. This site is very organized and full of information.

These sites are subject to change. Go to your favorite search engine and type in Rain Forest for more sites.

Pass It On

Rain Forest Enthusiasts: educate readers around the country by passing on information you've learned about rain forests. Share your little-known facts and interesting stories. Tell others about animals, insects, or people of the rain forest. We want to hear from you!

To get posted on the ABDO Publishing Company website E-mail us at
"Science@abdopub.com"
Visit the ABDO Publishing Company website at www.abdopub.com

Index